I trust you ~~~~~~~
to read as it was ~~~~
great quotes, and quick-to-the-point ~~~~
on the goals of the day, which got me to thinking and that ~~~~
resulted in this healthcare marketing and sales book providing a
daily dose of education, inspiration and motivation.

Each day comes with new opportunities and this book, one day
at a time, provides a new message on leadership, motivation,
sales strategy and more.

And just like all the fabulous representatives working in the field
every day, this book is designed to be fun and inspirational. A
huge shout out to all the physician relations representatives who
work hard to improve their skills and make their organization a
better place because of the work they do. This book is for you.

Healthcare has its challenges, but it is still the best place in the
world to work. I acknowledge the team at Barlow/McCarthy for
the marvelous work they do to support our clients.

After daydreaming about this book idea, I met with another
author, Paul Bailey. Paul's earlier book, *366 Days of Excellence*
was my starting point and I am grateful for his support in
creating the path.

Dave Paulus provided the perfect book cover and I am thankful
for his exceptional graphic design talent.

Ashley Graw a young, talented marketer gave me a tremendous
advantage in making this concept a reality. She worked endless
hours as we reviewed and revised content and determined how
to best present it. It was marvelous to work with an exceptionally
talented and motivated person.

Forward Thinking

Today is the most marvelous of days. We have the perfect setting from which to rid ourselves of the failures of this past year and reach to create a magnificent new beginning.

JANUARY 1

Attitude

Don't ever befriend blame. It often comes
in the form of pain you bear because others
are not supporting your efforts. While it gives
momentary solace, it is not your ally. If you become
accustomed to blame, it will take up residence in
your approach and almost be impossible to evict.
Believe you are strong enough to sell around it.

JANUARY 2

Great Messages

It is unlikely that anyone can be an "expert" on relationships since we are always in a state of learning. The minute you believe you have the relationship and resulting sales approach mastered, is the minute you become vulnerable to errors, mistakes in judgment, and failure.

JANUARY 3

Strategic Sales

Be ready, willing and able to educate and inform.
Prospects may not know you, what you represent,
or what your role to support them is. It is your
responsibility to inform them so they understand
your value to them. Remember, their station is
always tuned to WIIFM – What's In It For Me.

JANUARY 4

Competition

The competition consumes a great deal of energy. It's often helpful to consider what they provide and then how much impact it is having on the decision process. Assuming you are in a market where the competitor is working to earn new referrals, are you on offense or defense?

Forward Thinking

Lofty goals and desire are fabulous, but you need more. Work every day to harness internal support, find a new nugget of knowledge, and try a new approach. When your efforts move in the direction of your desires, you are able to reach your goals.

JANUARY 6

Motivation

Be careful of prescribing too much to the "wish principle"--- addressing sales expectations by "wishing" them to exist. Wishes are simply gifts of permission by which representatives placate deficiencies and limitations with delusions of grandeur. Problems can't be wished away and sales situations can't be wished to success. Determine what you need to work on and get it done.

JANUARY 7

Forward Thinking

Encourage your relationship sales team to gather information for leaders and to provide regular exchange about the topic with prospects. Present the details in a way that gets the leader's attention.

JANUARY 8

Strategic Sales

The role of the representative in service delivery is to properly position the products and services, to gather objective details about what went wrong when the service was not delivered as promised, and to represent the team and its members in the most positive light.

JANUARY 9

Great Messages

Let go of the need to talk and your sales relationships will improve. Never believe you can control what another person thinks or wants. We can only guide them through questions, then offer insights and guidance based on their needs.

JANUARY 10

Internal Relationships

The greatest gift you can give to your organization is to be a person with the highest standard of credibility. You don't turn it off and on like a faucet – using it only when you need it – it is a full- time responsibility. It is to be the "divining rod" of truth. Credibility is hard to earn. It is also easy to lose, so think about what would turn the tide for you.

JANUARY 11

Leadership

Make work fun. When you have oversight for a group of people who are gregarious, there is an almost mandatory obligation to lighten things up every now and again. Most field representatives are pushing hard to meet their weekly demands. Showing respect and recognition will go a long way to maintaining their motivation and momentum. The boss who can remind them they are valued, do something spontaneous, or make everyone laugh, is a welcome addition.

JANUARY 12

Strategic Sales

Find a great tidbit of helpful information to share.
Conversations start the process.

Attitude

Sales character is not a facade. It is the individual's personal spirit as they represent themselves and the organization in the marketplace over the long-term. Our character is the life-force which steers us to our great victories, and pushes us toward excellence.

JANUARY 14

Great Messages

Whenever you start a conversation around the topic of sales, a couple of key questions inevitably arise: "Are you really selling?" and "Why do they need to be sold?" Craft a good definition of sales for your market, and use it often. Acceptance begins with education.

Internal Relationships

Help your internal stakeholders understand that dumping the bucket does not earn relationships or referrals. Message management is a key part of relationship sales, in part because of the pace, the variety of communication tools and the unpredictable nature of the market. More is not always better.

JANUARY 16

Attitude

The greatest sales relationships are the ones which encourage you to assume the lead when it is appropriate. Power, which should flow freely between people, is the oil in the machinery of great relationship sales.

JANUARY 17

Strategic Sales

Is your approach the same for most prospects? If you find you're connecting better with one type of prospect, it may be that you are matched best to one personality type. Invest in learning about DISC -- or a similar tool -- and put personality into your sales practice.

JANUARY 18

Focus

We learn so much from the words that represent this day: Vision, Success, Commitment, and Focus. Reflect upon them, personalize them, and determine a way to embrace each one today. Visualize what success is, commit to it, focus on it, and you will succeed.

JANUARY 19

Strategic Sales

Success -- the ability to exceed expectations -- is found in the understanding of personal strengths along with weaknesses and limitations. Personally assess where you are and use the knowledge to grow your strengths.

JANUARY 20

Great Messages

Getting in the door is only half the battle. Representatives at best-practice organizations provide depth during the early visits to allow for a professional exchange. Get to this level and you'll be welcomed back on a regular basis. First impressions count.

JANUARY 21

Attitude

Relationship sales have never been the easiest path to travel. It is filled with the pitfalls of operational challenges, competitive threats and some clients who just can't be pleased. While they can challenge your spirit, stay strong.

JANUARY 22

Impact

While there are volumes of books that purport to offer best methods to close, some are so gimmicky they most likely would result in embarrassment if used. Stick to a standard approach. Be confident, summarize the needs, confirm their interest and talk about the next steps.

Strategic Sales

Representatives who are working to earn referrals from physicians will be more successful when they gain insights into the type of patients the physician refers. This is not just a diagnosis. What else can you learn about their patients and the practice?

JANUARY 24

Leadership

Great leaders motivate and challenge
others only to the extent they motivate and
challenge themselves.

JANUARY 25

Internal Relationships

Teams committed to success fill their positions
with people of integrity that "walk the talk."
How will you demonstrate this on behalf of your
organization today?

JANUARY 26

Forward Thinking

Do you have the momentum to deepen the relationship? Long-term relationships are so special, yet they can get stale if there is no energy and commitment to keep them fresh.

Strategic Sales

It is a commonly accepted fact that it is far more costly to find new business than it is to maintain your current referral sources. Beyond taking the time to listen to their concerns, what is your strategy for adding value for your loyal clients?

JANUARY 28

Attitude

Character teaches us that each one of us,
regardless of our position, or status, has a
responsibility to our relationships and our
organizations in making them grow and succeed.

JANUARY 29

Forward Thinking

Become a person who can always envision great
things for yourself and others. While you can be
committed to small victories, you must never be
completely satisfied with the level you are at.
Always strive for even greater heights of success.

JANUARY 30

Great Messages

Some have been programmed to believe it's enough to ask for the business. It's not. Spend your time learning and developing the personal tools needed to connect and build relationships instead of waiting for results. The sooner everyone understands that it's about the client, the sooner we all benefit from success.

JANUARY 31

Competition

Moving business from a competing organization
means that you must have a clear approach
for advancing the relationship. Stay focused on
moving deeper in the discussion about their needs
and where you think the next actionable step will
be for them.

Great Messages

Listen and provide details about relevant services and offerings. Never think you are just there to gather intelligence. The client must sense your first priority is to create relationships.

FEBRUARY 2

Strategic Sales

Crisis sales is exhausting. You must never place immediate impulse sales execution issues ahead of your organizational sales strategy. Failure to follow this process fosters the inability for significant long-term change or growth to occur.

FEBRUARY 3

Internal Relationships

As changes occur in staffing and priorities, an
internal communication plan is an excellent way to
keep your physician strategy front and center for
those who need to support it.

FEBRUARY 4

Strategic Sales

Exceed expectations. It's sort of like the TV game show, "The Price is Right." If you underbid, even by a lot, you're in the game. But if you are just $1 over, you're out of the game. If you under promise and over deliver, you're still in the game. Overpromise and underperform? Game over.

FEBRUARY 5

Forward Thinking

Do not limit yourself to achieving only big victories.
Be capable of winning small sales and stay
focused on earning a little bit at a time. It will get
you to the same place.

FEBRUARY 6

Competition

Winners learn valuable lessons when they lose.
There are times when the near term opportunity
does not come to fruition. Always leave the door
open to future opportunity. Be gracious, learn from
the experience and move on.

FEBRUARY 7

Attitude

Four emotional traits are needed to facilitate significant change at a personal sales level. They are: commitment, passion, persistence and self-trust. Without these tools, the process of change becomes as harrowing a task as going over Niagara Falls in a barrel.

Great Messages

You can't be successful in sales if you can't get by the gatekeeper. Script your message. And practice your scripted message. If it sounds natural you will be invited in, not kept out.

FEBRUARY 9

Strategic Sales

Create a welcoming environment. Style, presence,
types of questions, and types of answers --
they all have the power to welcome, offend or
create tension.

FEBRUARY 10

Internal Relationships

The best way to create external success is to create internal success. You will not be able to travel down the road of sales success without a successful team to back up your field efforts.

FEBRUARY 11

Leadership

A leader's job can be broken down into three major categories. The first, defined as organizational or administrative, is concerned with the necessary tedium of bureaucratic process, i.e. paperwork, which is a requirement for efficient and effective teams. The second category is preparation. This is the developmental process for teaching skills and systems. The third category is sales execution, whereby you lead the team into competition. An effective leader must be able to handle these three tasks. They cannot be delegated to someone else. Accept the reality of the job and work to your ability.

FEBRUARY 12

Great Messages

One of the greatest gifts you can give a prospect/
physician is to publicly recognize them for what they
have done, or what they mean to you. In contrast,
one of the surest ways to irreparably damage a
relationship is to criticize them in front of others.

FEBRUARY 13

Impact

Be flexible. We generally feel like we are always the flexible ones and we'd like the prospects to be a bit more pliable themselves. Be sure about that -- and be flexible.

Great Messages

Respect is something you earn with words and actions of integrity, which show and tell the client that you are worthy. Never forget to give clients the respect they deserve. We reap best what we sow selflessly.

FEBRUARY 15

Attitude

Everything you do in your sales relationships must be considered in contributing to the ultimate success for your prospect as well as yourself and your organization. Create win-win messages for each constituent.

Great Messages

The ability to actively engage in a conversation
with comments, questions, and perhaps
clarification statements, is both art and science.
Great sales people work at making sales
interactions comfortable.

Strategic Sales

Risk is an essential component of every successful sales person. You can never achieve lofty goals without placing yourself beyond the safe and secure patterns of the past. Rewards require taking risks. Try to take a new risk today with your sales strategy.

FEBRUARY 18

Attitude

A battle rages inside sales people. It is a battle between doubt and faith. Doubt is the resident monster in our mind. It likes to remind us that maybe, just maybe, we are not capable of sales success. Faith is our supportive companion telling us that we can, and will be successful. Never lose your faith, or let doubt overshadow it.

FEBRUARY 19

Focus

Be willing and able to live a life of character.
Character keeps us steady. It keeps us humble.
And it keeps us focused. Character allows us to
examine our own issues while keeping an eye on
how our growth impacts the greater whole.

FEBRUARY 20

Attitude

In sales we always hope that the client has honest intentions. By doing all we can to support the growth and success of the client and their needs, we show ourselves to be persons of character in that relationship.

FEBRUARY 21

Internal Relationships

When internal problems arise, it is best if they are confronted immediately. When issues linger, they tend to worsen and it becomes hard for a team to recover without doing damage to the relationship.

Strategic Sales

Empathy is a wonderful characteristic for relationship sales. Empathetic people naturally work to understand the needs of the other person, and they work hard to listen and learn. Does this describe you? Remember to leverage that attribute to earn growth.

FEBRUARY 23

Motivation

Sales success requires endless evaluation in terms of where you are now, where you have been, and what you did -- or didn't do -- to move that distance and direction.

Strategic Sales

Representatives who are driven to achieve new skills are able to try new methods and learn from the process. Success and failure go hand-in-hand as you test new concepts and approaches. Change and growth is challenging for the sales representative, both physically and mentally. Treat yourself with kindness and patience during this time. Be realistic about the pace of change. Live the pursuit of success one day at a time.

FEBRUARY 25

Leadership

Lead when you need to. Follow when you must.
Encourage at all times. Stay focused.

FEBRUARY 26

Great Messages

Always start your sales call with your intent,
including the reason for the meeting and agenda.
Then give the prospect the opportunity to share
their agenda if it is different.

FEBRUARY 27

Attitude

A healthy relationship sales representative exudes warmth. A healthy relationship thrives in an environment where all are accepted for whom they are and, as a result, feel safe.

Competition

Let's face it, one of the reasons many physician relations programs exist is because of competitive forces at work in your market. To be successful in earning new referrals you must sell against competitors.

FEBRUARY 29

Strategic Sales

Identify the influential group of physicians you can't afford to lose, find a way to ensure they have -- in addition to the representative -- a strong connection to a leader in the organization.

MARCH 1

Great Messages

Working with physicians, there is a very real obligation to create clear, consistent and distinct messages.

MARCH 2

Forward Thinking

The essence of momentum is a can-do attitude. But momentum is not just high emotion or people doing the right thing, although all of that is good and contributes. Momentum is tangible – is yours?

MARCH 3

Strategic Sales

Learning how to sell the right way takes a great deal of time and practice, yet it ultimately gives you a rich and rewarding relationship that works best for our type of selling. Never let the passion for quick-fix victories overshadow the goal of long term dialogue-based relationship sales.

MARCH 4

Great Messages

Successful representatives use dialogue to understand what prospects need and provide insights and data to paint a mental picture of the reasons why prospects should use a particular organization.

MARCH 5

Competition

It is really important to clarify who is a competitor and why. There are always the obvious competitors, but don't stop there. Know them all, but do not let them define who you are, or how you approach the market.

MARCH 6

Internal Relationships

With relationship sales calls targeted at prospects, there is a definite advantage to having sales and operations in sync. Take a step forward to initiate a better relationship.

MARCH 7

Great Messages

Creative ideas give you opportunities to connect.

MARCH 8

Impact

Solve problems quickly and, if you can, tell them when and why. Anyone who has ever done field sales will have examples of the impact this has, both positive and negative. The "slow no" is history. Prospects won't tolerate it and will find other options.

MARCH 9

Forward Thinking

Personal growth requires you to do three things: Take the time to learn about your team and company. Process the steps needed to achieve the goals. And determine how you will succeed in showing measured growth.

MARCH 10

Competition

Determine which competing organizations the prospect is using and then consider all the ways to differentiate your facility to earn the business. If you put a competitive strategy in writing, your efforts will be more successful.

MARCH 11

Attitude

Did you ever realize there are two words hidden in the word believe? One is be and the other is live. On the road to sales success it is quite possible for us to lose our way. When we do, we should listen to the voice telling us to return to the most basic principles. Focus on the role we were hired to do and believe in ourselves. When we get lost, we must believe. We must be, and we must live.

Great Messages

Trust and trustworthiness in the sales process requires that the client is being honest with you, and that, in turn, you are being completely honest and truthful with them.

Leadership

Good work habits are the underpinning for any position, but monitoring work performance is much easier to do in the office than outside it. The best managers find creative methods and design systematic tools to keep apprised of their team's level of effectiveness in the field.

MARCH 14

Great Messages

There are many ways from which an individual or team gets to the top. Some are ethical, some are not. I believe there is only one way to get and stay on top. To do so requires that a person be driven to do the right thing. They must be committed to success and willing to constantly examine the tough questions.

MARCH 15

Internal Relationships

Constantly work on improving internal communication. Never allow the adage -- "out of sight-out of mind" -- describe you.

MARCH 16

Attitude

No excuses. It is very easy to lay the blame on issues perceived to be outside your control. Once this type of reasoning is allowed to be part of your conversation with a prospect, you provide an automatic "out" and lose momentum to work around the situation.

MARCH 17

Strategic Sales

Differentiation and drive are keys to success.
Consider where you excel and leverage this.

MARCH 18

Great Messages

To earn your way past the gatekeeper, make certain you have a reason to visit. It might be that your internal stakeholder wanted to gain feedback from you, or you wanted to share information about a new service, or you wanted to follow up on a specific topic from the last call. Find a good reason to be there. Otherwise, don't go.

MARCH 19

Focus

Learn to find strength in solitude. Take time to be
by yourself and focus your thoughts on the tasks
ahead of you. We must tackle our greatest sales
challenges ourselves. Prepare yourself. Do a pre-
plan, but also practice quiet visioning to see the
call and your success.

MARCH 20

Great Messages

When the prospect tells you about a problem with one of your competitors, don't criticize or emphasize, but rather open the door of opportunity by asking one question: "Has it gotten to the place where you'd consider another solution?" If their answer is no, you won't benefit from pushing your service in the prospect's direction. Timing is everything, stay the course.

MARCH 21

Strategic Sales

Be committed to healthy, functional sales relationships. Two fundamental questions provide the litmus test. Does the relationship help my organization and my prospect? Am I doing all I can in this relationship to ensure a win-win environment of trust, candor and added value?

MARCH 22

Great Messages

We connect best with those who are like us.
Listen to the word choice from the prospect, it
will advance the relationship if you can provide
summary statements that use their words and feel
familiar.

Motivation

Being committed to sales success requires you to do your very best at all times. While you may not possess all the skills or necessary knowledge, always keep trying and never give up without a fight. You may not earn every sale you undertake, but never lose by being outworked. Let resolve and persistence be your rallying cries.

MARCH 24

Strategic Sales

Targeting the right prospects is essential for success. Don't set sales targets based only on intuition. Start by considering what you will sell, use data to assess past referral patterns, consider real growth potential, know where they currently refer and make certain you can differentiate your service in a positive way. Are your targets the right ones?

MARCH 25

Internal Relationships

Create your messages. Good messages focus on expectations that will be consistently met. Take the time to think about the messages that will give you more confidence in your tone and less likelihood of overpromising.

MARCH 26

Strategic Sales

No sales or relationship succeeds and grows with shortcuts and manipulation of people, ideals and beliefs. "All is fair in love and war" is not a phrase that fits, or supports, relationship sales.

MARCH 27

Forward Thinking

Craft a plan that helps you understand areas where you're losing momentum. Begin a dialogue to understand the emotional and business reasons for this. You will not overcome their concerns if you do not understand the emotional side of the referral decisions.

MARCH 28

Great Messages

The best programs are focused on building relationships through regular, face-to-face visits between representatives and their prospects. It's almost that simple. To earn new referrals, it's not enough to know what the prospect needs. You must also recognize that the business we want currently goes somewhere else. For representatives to gain those referrals, they need to go beyond simply telling them what you offer. Best-practice organizations position their differences, gain the physicians' trust, and earn the opportunity to care for the referred patients.

MARCH 29

Attitude

There are times when the pressure to succeed
mounts and creates so much stress you want to
quit. When this happens the only course of action
is to search deep down inside yourself and find one
more ounce of resolve and the strength to continue.
Fatigue and failure are not necessarily your
enemies. They are, in fact, not so subtle reminders
that you are on the path to eventual success.

MARCH 30

Leadership

As an internal leader you need to respect the nature of the representative's relationship with the physician-client.

APRIL 1

Attitude

Character plays a large role in our ability to communicate successfully. Respect what the client is saying or has said. By treating them with respect, you establish trust and understanding without fear of being judged for what they say or feel.

APRIL 2

Strategic Sales

You will be more impactful when you customize and personalize the message. For the most part, the office staff is interested in access, so focus your messages to them on the attributes that describe how to implement.

APRIL 3

Impact

Create a formal process for talking about
challenges before they occur. This may be
an issue within the sales area or within the
organization. The best crisis planning happens
before the crisis.

APRIL 4

Great Messages

The greatest enemy of our growth is, and will always be, us. We can do more mental sabotage in our personal drive for success than any outsider could ever dream of doing. The first step in any master plan for success should be found in our ability to control the demons of failure which live in our heads.

APRIL 5

Internal Relationships

The field team is a living example of the organization's brand. Brand identity at a personal level is about style and approach. Consider your overall style. Does it match the organization?

APRIL 6

Strategic Sales

Knowledge is one key to personal sales growth and the ability to change referral patterns. The more knowledge we possess the more likely our ability to differentiate our products and services.

Great Messages

Nobody wants to hear a sales pitch. And if you're doing all the telling, it's a pitch. Monitor your calls today. How much time are you telling?

APRIL 8

Attitude

As you drive down the road of sales success, treat all people with dignity, honor and respect – at all times. "What comes around, goes around" is a harsh reality you don't want to experience. You never know when a person you treated badly will be the person you will need later on. The same people you meet on the way up the ladder are the ones you meet going down. Learn to make allies. Who should you reach out to today?

APRIL 9

Focus

It's not just about what worked yesterday. Continue to innovate, find new approaches, and test new scripts. Some may not work, but some will be marvelous new techniques for your sales success tool kit.

APRIL 10

Forward Thinking

When a tree is attacked by relentless winds,
it responds to the threat by growing its roots
deeper for greater strength and stability. When
you are challenged by those around you, you
must learn to set your roots in an iron will and an
uncompromising belief in yourself and your goals.

APRIL 11

Great Messages

Less is more with gatekeepers. From the gatekeeper's perspective, the essence of the conversation is to rule you out. Stop talking before you give them a reason to do so.

APRIL 12

Motivation

Consider the need for prospects to grow their own business. There has to be some gain for them. If not, they won't be interested in changing their patterns. Take the time to jot down what you perceive to be your prospects' motivators before you make your visits today.

APRIL 13

Strategic Sales

Select those prospects that can send more referrals your way. It's logical, but often not done to the extent it could be. Review the list with an open mind and if it was created using hunches, then find the data to help ground your efforts.

APRIL 14

Forward Thinking

Create your vision. Define your mission. Define the principles of your sales success. Establish your "code." And commit yourself to success – today, tomorrow and all the days ahead.

APRIL 15

Competition

Opinions differ on the value of talking about a competitor to learn what they do well. I'm confident I already have a sense of what they do. I prefer to not give up any of my short time with a prospect to listen to the attributes of my competition.

APRIL 16

Strategic Sales

Numbers sell. The ability to use numbers to demonstrate the impact of our efforts is a powerful tool.

APRIL 17

Impact

Appreciate physicians and the work they do. Don't gush at them but do show them you value them through actions and works.

APRIL 18

Internal Relationships

All team members must not only learn the art of "being," but also master the art of "being with" other people. A team will only succeed in direct relation to its willingness to change and grow in a unified manner.

APRIL 19

Attitude

You can't be all things to all people. Instead, try to be something substantial for yourself. That in turn gives you the internal tenacity for sales success.

APRIL 20

Forward Thinking

Great sales people are always willing to try once more. Today is your day to go after the prospect you've been avoiding.

APRIL 21

Attitude

Commit yourself to be remembered as a "loyal" individual. Never turn your back on your organization; it just does not get you anything positive at a work or personal level. Instead focus on how they have invested in you. Loyalty is important when successfully representing your organization's products and services.

APRIL 22

Great Messages

What makes for great dialogue? It's mutual interest in the topic, shared conversation and great listening. Without all three, you're missing the mark.

APRIL 23

Internal Relationships

Work to earn expert positioning within the organization. Offer objective, timely, and meaningful information that demonstrates your expertise. Keep in mind you lose the advantage in a heartbeat if you pretend to be an expert in something you are not. Carve out your niche area of expertise and use the power and information very wisely.

APRIL 24

Strategic Sales

Remember those customers who know you best really do have more issues. They are invested; it is your gift that they share, it is your gift to take action. The right action internally, while it may be painful at times, is always the right thing to do.

APRIL 25

Strategic Sales

Take advantage of cumulative knowledge that is learned from individual members of the team. Leverage phrases and insights that work for others when you script communication. If you have a challenging prospect, brainstorm options and then try one of the ideas.

APRIL 26

Leadership

You must be confident if you say someone from the organization will address the prospect's concern that they will respond in a timely manner. Senior leaders have the clout to make that happen.

APRIL 27

Forward Thinking

Just wanting referrals is not enough to get them.
Be realistic as you evaluate growth potential. Make
sure you have a clear sense of the impact when
they shift their business. Look beyond-the-numbers
to patterns in their individual and group referrals.
Measurement is a very big deal.

APRIL 28

Strategic Sales

There is a tremendous opportunity to connect with prospects as long as your topic is relevant and your message is on point.

APRIL 29

Attitude

Displaying your selling character is not a part-time act. You don't perform in one role and then ignore that relationship style at other times. Be genuine and be your best self.

Great Messages

Recognize that the most loyal users of your product or service will always have complaints. They love you enough to whine! Be grateful. Listen, learn, acknowledge and appreciate them.

Strategic Sales

No one finds sales success by accident. It is a by-product of careful strategy, thoughtful planning, tireless commitment and unwavering belief in your organization and its services.

MAY 2

Motivation

You are making a difference. Write down a difference you made for someone recently. It could be a client, a team mate, an internal stakeholder or your leader. Take the time to reflect on the good things you do.

MAY 3

Great Messages

While product and sales knowledge are essential tools, never forget to also let your instincts guide you. Sometimes we don't have the time to think through our responses when selling. If you trust yourself, then let yourself go. You just might amaze yourself at what you can contribute when the heat is on.

MAY 4

Leadership

Reward the positive. Rejection is common on the job, so the best managers find positives and recognize them. Working with gatekeepers, sitting in a practice for an hour only to have the doctor get called to deliver a baby, or stepping out of the air conditioned car in August heat and humidity is not glamorous. In addition, those who are good at their jobs add a full dose of pressure on themselves to keep up the pace.

MAY 5

Attitude

Never be envious or jealous of other people's
achievements or accomplishments. There is no
greater drain on your capacity to succeed than
these two emotions.

MAY 6

Strategic Sales

What is your "point of difference?" What does your organization have in place to earn new business? What is going to set you and your organization apart from the competition? If you don't know, you can't sell it.

Impact

Never fear being told "No" because it provides you the opportunity for dialogue. Simply and gently ask, "Why not?" Their reply will enable you to understand their needs and what you need to do to re-open the door.

MAY 8

Forward Thinking

What is your organization doing to ensure business earned is business that you keep? Formalize your new client approach to ensure there's attention to details of service delivery. Make sure the client's personal and professional goals are detailed and a plan is in place to exceed expectations.

MAY 9

Attitude

Celebrate the differences we all possess. We grow
in our relationships -- and our sales success --
when people offer new perspectives to our mind's
eye. Accept others and the unique gifts they bring
to your relationships with them.

MAY 10

Internal Relationships

The most successful sales representatives understand that sales are only successful when there is an ability to deliver on the promise. Victory is achieved as a whole.

MAY 11

Strategic Sales

If the representative cannot show the prospect the value of spending time with them, the prospect won't find the time to meet. And it's not just losing scheduled appointments. Soon, even casual hallway connections will go away. Gone are the days when prospects had time to politely listen, regardless of their level of interest, or to list all of the problems at the organization, especially if they feel that they have shared them before to no avail.

MAY 12

Forward Thinking

Concern yourself with yourself. Take care of
issues in your own backyard. Don't spend time
and energy in trying to fix others, or find their
faults and limitations. There is no greater wedge
in a relationship than one person being a self-
appointed critic.

MAY 13

Impact

As you earn success in sales, never forget where
you have been, and the people who assisted
you. Be grateful for their wisdom; and consider
those things you perhaps did not want to hear.
Your success was further enhanced because you
listened. Be grateful and tell them thank you the
first chance you get.

MAY 14

Strategic Sales

Make sure there are no precluding circumstances (e.g. payer mix or patient preference) that would have an impact on your ability to encourage the prospect to send more referrals to you.

Attitude

Change and growth occur when the natural law of personal capacity understands that we now posses the skills needed to move in a forward direction.

MAY 16

Focus

We've all heard that enthusiasm is contagious. Can the same be said for passion and focus? How do you demonstrate these attributes as you make your calls?

Competition

Good competitive strategy means that we make good business decisions when there is an opportunity to take business from the competing provider. It is the representative's job to understand the level of satisfaction with a competing product and determine if there is an emotional connection that complicates the ability to earn the business.

MAY 18

Attitude

Credibility is your tool to earn trust. And make no mistake, trust must be earned. Consider steps you'll use to earn credibility with a new prospect. What's in your tool kit to reinforce it with existing clients and earn it with prospects?

MAY 19

Strategic Sales

Our ultimate growth and success are dependent upon our ability to support the practice in growth and success. One shining example of how to earn long-term relationships can be summed up in six words: Never take more than you give.

MAY 20

Internal Relationships

The work environment's culture will either hinder or enhance internal communication. Does your culture allow for internal communication to happen freely?

MAY 21

Focus

Set realistic expectations for the type and amount of growth you want to see in your organization. Changing referral patterns takes time, so make certain a focused and consistent series of messages is in place for the representative to move forward in earning new business.

MAY 22

Strategic Sales

It's a great day to inventory your sales tools.
Assess what you're using and then score with
relevance and impact.

MAY 23

Great Messages

It's your job -- not the prospect's -- to engage in conversation. Many prospects just go to their mental "happy place" as you talk. Engage them, involve them, listen to them and earned results will follow.

MAY 24

Forward Thinking

There is no greater day of opportunity than the one you have today. Don't delay the pursuit of a sale until tomorrow. Seize the day.

MAY 25

Great Messages

Assure the gatekeeper of his or her wisdom. When you get an appointment set up, let them know you appreciate their help and the time with the prospect will be beneficial and productive.

MAY 26

Great Messages

A sales call is only a valuable tool for a prospect if it is customized with a personal message tailored to the prospect's needs. The representative needs – at every level – to determine how to ask good questions to learn about each prospect's specific interests and provide information that is relevant to them.

MAY 27

Attitude

Have a genuine concern for the well-being and
growth of those in the practice. One of the best
ways to find personal happiness comes from
assisting others in their quest for peace, happiness
and satisfaction. It also enhances sales success.

MAY 28

Strategic Sales

The best way to understand the implications of growth is to have an ongoing relationship with the data, or the person who works with the data. Be proactive with this and keep selling internally -- it is such a difference maker.

MAY 29

Great Messages

Learn through listening. When representatives are learning about a new service or product, they should ask lots of detailed questions to clearly understand the product's scope and availability. Record the product questions you learn today.

MAY 30

Attitude

Be a representative capable of empathy. Empathy
is the ability to place yourself in someone else's
shoes. Empathy should not be confused with
sympathy, which is the ability to feel sorrow or
compassion for the client's misfortunes. Are you
too sympathetic? To take the time and completely
comprehend what the client is feeling without
taking sides against your organization is very
important.

MAY 31

Internal Relationships

Sometimes representatives waste valuable time trying to create an aura of effectiveness and value without really having the internal power to make things happen. Learn the inside perspective, know the type of field intelligence that gets attention and you'll own the aura.

JUNE 1

Strategic Sales

Successful growth requires acceptance that lasting change can be a slow, arduous process. We can overcome this by understanding what we need to change in short-term benchmarks, and strategically planning to address those future needs in a linear fashion.

Focus

At the start of a new relationship, the focus should not necessarily be on an immediate sale. Good relationship sales cannot begin until there is a clear understanding of the prospect and his or her needs. Gaining a commitment for more referrals comes as a result of demonstrating how the product or service can support the customer's need. Do it right; start with their needs. Don't just dump the bucket.

JUNE 3

Forward Thinking

Think ahead. Instead of only thinking about the goals for the week, create a short-run vs. long-run goal for each prospect. Live today with an eye on tomorrow.

JUNE 4

Focus

Your sales success is dependent upon your clarity of purpose, consistency of approach and your focus. Simple to say, difficult to do.

JUNE 5

Strategic Sales

Explore the type of business that the prospect can and will shift to your organization. Rather than telling prospects about your offerings, create two good questions to learn more about the prospect's needs. What questions are the most beneficial to the prospects you are visiting today?

JUNE 6

Motivation

Commit yourself to perform three little tasks. Learn to say "Good job-Well done" to others especially when they have gone the extra mile for you. Learn to pat others on the back when they need it. And be a leader by mentoring others.

JUNE 7

Great Messages

Think about strategic factors that may have implications for your prospects. What's happening in the marketplace that could be affecting their perspectives?

JUNE 8

Strategic Sales

The indifferent prospect is the most challenging as they have no perceived need for your product or service. If you're meeting with one of them today, make certain you've done your homework and that you know the differences in your service, and the advantage they have, over their existing provider.

JUNE 9

Great Messages

Never consider one of your responsibilities in a relationship is to cure another person of their problems.

JUNE 10

Internal Relationships

Sales teams consist of people and their relationships. If the team is to achieve success, all must be committed to excellence at the individual and interpersonal level.

Strategic Sales

Sometimes we find ourselves with people in practices we do not like. It's a reality of our world. There is no magic formula that can make people like each other. In fact, representatives do not have to be proponents of a "love fest" to be successful.

JUNE 12

Great Messages

Relationship selling is more about discovering prospect's needs. To change physicians' referral patterns you must remember that people in general are resistant to change. To earn trust you must listen for nuggets of information which will position you to solve their problems.

JUNE 13

Forward Thinking

The formula for healthy sales communication is quite simple: Listen more, speak less, be open, be honest, be trustworthy, be knowledgeable, be realistic, be focused, be brief, be flexible, and work at it -- work at it -- work at it.

JUNE 14

Attitude

In the pursuit of victories and success never forget to have some fun along the way. Enjoy the journey.

JUNE 15

Internal Relationships

It is important that all members have a vested interest in the success of the sales effort. With this you create alignment – all members on the same page, working toward a unified goal, which supports the personal, departmental and organizational goals. Simply put: the members support the growth of the organization, and the organization supports its individual's sales success.

JUNE 16

Great Messages

Communication has a crucial role in sales. The messages you send must be clearly understood and the same is true for the messages you receive.

JUNE 17

Strategic Sales

Step back, assess where you are, and set some program development goals along with your outcome goals. After all, we all know that there are challenges with keeping these sales efforts on course. An essential ingredient is indentifying what "on course" is.

JUNE 18

Forward Thinking

Until you have achieved perfection, let others
live their lives as they see fit. Work with them and
provide support, but not criticism. If they ask,
then share but be careful. The sales psyche can
be fragile.

JUNE 19

Attitude

One of the most desired components of any sales relationship is respect. While we want it so very badly, it is also something which can be difficult for us to give internally. Seek out someone within your organization that would benefit from your demonstrated respect today.

JUNE 20

Great Messages

Growing business is a lot like growing your garden. It benefits from a good plan, but won't grow if no seeds are planted or tended. The cultivated plan should result in a bountiful harvest. Which part of gardening do you do best?

JUNE 21

Internal Relationships

It is so easy to be a close-knit sales team when you are winning. Therein lies one of the great paradoxes found in our sales teams: You don't win to find unity. You find unity to be successful.

JUNE 22

Strategic Sales

There is a tremendous value in the concept of visualization, especially where sales success is concerned. Establish and embrace the mental image of yourself succeeding. Hold on to this picture with all your might. Don't let it disappear from your view. By creating a positive image of yourself, you provide the opportunity for the vision to become fact. Self-fulfilling prophecy is a positive force.

JUNE 23

Focus

Focus is about looking at the reason for the organization's service/products and then assessing which prospects to target. How should the prospect be targeted, and when will the goal be met? Plan it. See it. Do it.

JUNE 24

Attitude

Give a compliment to a physician, a service leader,
or someone who makes your life, or the life of a
patient better.

JUNE 25

Competition

Credibility is the foremost competitive differentiator. We like to be with people who we enjoy and who make us comfortable. Creating good rapport gives you the opportunity to have the kind of discussion necessary to understand their needs and what it would take to earn the business.

JUNE 26

Impact

It is our responsibility as sales representatives to constantly and consistently be willing to examine our directions and strive to be all we can be. The very acts of doing this will ensure and increase our standards.

Personalize your message with the interests of the physician in mind. Make a statement with those things that you need to make sure the client sees. It's strategic selling.

JUNE 27

Strategic Sales

Problems are a fact of life -- sad but true. Gather objective details when the service is not delivered as promised. While you can take the first step and be proactive, there must be a commitment to service delivery on both sides. Take a customer point of view. It is critically important that we step back and assess the current environment for them and with them and then craft the right approach.

JUNE 28

Impact

Great sales people are great listeners. When people are listened to, they feel important and confident their input will help shape the solution. How can you demonstrate great listening today?

JUNE 29

Attitude

I can never be something you want me to be. I can only be the person I need to be. Who do you need to be?

JUNE 30

Leadership

Leaders can help by sharing the type of information they find valuable and understanding that there is a careful balance between learning and heavy probing. Always remember to maintain the long-term relationship.

JULY 1

Strategic Sales

Call out your best personal tools today. Knowledge and communication skills create the opportunity for more referrals.

JULY 2

Internal Relationships

Any sales vision must be respectful of the internal team. As much as you may desire it, others may not understand what you are trying to do. They are not trying to defeat you; they simply need patience and encouragement so they recognize your growth efforts will not be done at their expense. Show them that the results you are earning will enhance the organization's success.

JULY 3

Strategic Sales

Encourage more business from prospects that represent the level of quality your organization wants to achieve. The organization will benefit from objectifying the features of quality that come into play. Consider how you are determining their quality -- or are you just looking at the numbers?

JULY 4

Great Messages

Connect on a regular basis. Consistency is golden.
Have a plan for this or you will not be able to have
the same positive impact.

Impact

Recognize when prospects are ready to commit. They may ask questions about the process, or they may begin to talk about another resource and share what they were not providing that you indicated you could. Listen and watch body language, when they are interested, then you need to close.

JULY 6

Strategic Sales

Manage your portfolio. First determine the prospect's interests, and then stay on that topic until you convert them to new business. Think back over your last month, did you do this, or did you pitch different products each visit? Evaluate and adjust.

JULY 7

Attitude

It's your attitude that gets you through the rough spots and makes you successful. Nobody takes that away from you.

JULY 8

Great Messages

Assess the opportunity when the conversation is always about problems. A number of prospects may be perfectly content to wallow in complaints. Some don't want the situation to get better. All your efforts will not change their situation, recognize it and get resourceful in another direction.

JULY 9

Competition

Work the funnel, pre-plan for next steps assuming you get a nibble. Be prepared to offer people, data, or education. The more you are able to involve the client in your services and products, the greater your potential to earn those referrals.

JULY 10

Strategic Sales

A good physician relations representative can often gain clues and intelligence about a prospect's interest in a partnership or collaboration long before it becomes a formal request.

JULY 11

Forward Thinking

Never forget to temper your hard work with the notion of working efficiently. Too many representatives in the pursuit of success are defeated when they believe their goals are only about the amount of time and effort. They believe success is directly proportionate to the amount of hours spent. Be prepared – work with your brain, as well as your heart, as you learn to sell "smart."

JULY 12

Impact

Vow to leave each discussion with the prospect
feeling better about having met with you. It
requires a little pre-planning, but make certain that
at the end of your interaction you leave them with
a message or action that has them feeling like the
conversation was very worthwhile for them.

JULY 13

Great Messages

Any salesperson, in any relationship, must be able to do two things well in order for the communication process to take place. First; take the time and make the effort to truly listen to what is being said by the prospect. Second; deliver a message that contains both a factual component, as well as the proper emotional context. If you can master these two concepts then you have an opportunity to create a positive relationship and referral results.

JULY 14

Internal Relationships

There must always be balance to the negative feedback given to internal stakeholders. Failure to do so limits the meaning of the message, destroys credibility, and damages the program's effectiveness.

JULY 15

Attitude

Try not to let negativity get it in the way of your
dreams and goals. At the end of each day, train
yourself to let go of any animosity or ill will you
feel when things don't go your way. When you let
anger cripple your ability to function positively
in relationship sales or blind your greater
perspective, it has then become a problem which
you must solve to move forward.

JULY 16

Forward Thinking

Preparation is the key to consistent sales success. While you will get lucky and have a sales call go your way with limited planning, be honest and consider the missed opportunities.

JULY 17

Great Messages

Successful relationship building works only if you get focused time with the prospect. To have true sales success hone in on your skills to get past gatekeepers. Although not easy, it is possible. And frankly, it is not an option.

JULY 18

Focus

Did you ever stop to consider the uniqueness you offer to the world? There is only one "you" and we are all better for it. But don't let another person have to tell you that. Go out and live the special qualities you have, see the way you are capable. In doing so, you offer a gift to all.

JULY 19

Forward Thinking

The ability to be on time seems like such a
trivial concept to relationship sales. Yet it is
representative of your level of respect for another
person. If you are someone who is always late,
you must believe your time is more valuable and
important than anyone else's time. This is hardly a
platform for a healthy relationship to grow.

JULY 20

Strategic Sales

Quality is a great differentiator in positioning your product, but only if you can prove it. No one refers to poor quality so when you talk about quality give data driven examples of how you demonstrate quality.

JULY 21

Internal Relationships

Creativity is not a typical healthcare phenomenon. This means it's your job to introduce a need for trial and error with ideas and suggestions as you work to earn new referrals.

Attitude

Nobody likes to feel taken for granted. Make sure
your energy and commitment to current
users is high.

Strategic Sales

It is a fact that all the best sales plans are only as good as the ability to put those same plans into action.

JULY 24

Motivation

Don't look at your personal success as a sign of your brilliance. Consider what you do with your skills as the real measure. Offer your skills to others, provide insights to the internal stakeholders, get involved with your sales peers, and share the gifts.

JULY 25

Strategic Sales

Are you regularly tracking referral results that tie directly to your field efforts? Embrace the opportunity to show the value you add to the organization by measuring where you go, what you do and how you make a difference.

JULY 26

Attitude

Encourage new ideas by responding in a positive
light whenever you can, provide rationale and
details when you have to say no to a request.

Internal Relationships

What does a sales team need in each of its members? Representatives with a desire to earn business; people who face challenges with passion and resolve; people with a commitment to excellence; and individuals who hunger for personal growth and success for the organization. Build your pedigree.

JULY 28

Great Messages

Healthy communication is found in the capacity to take messages at face value. You must believe that there is no hidden meaning or agenda behind the message. Judge client communication fairly and equitably, and deliver them with the same spirit.

JULY 29

Strategic Sales

Life is filled with difficult decisions-decisions which ultimately determine the level of success we have in sales. We need to make those decisions with level-headed resolve, and with an understanding that making the proper decision improves our immediate sales success, enhances our relationships in the long-term, and contributes to the betterment of our organization.

JULY 30

Attitude

Courage is a critical attribute; it gives you the
ability to move past the world you now know.
It is a stepping stone for success in sales.
Success requires you to have the courage of your
convictions, and the courage to push yourself
forward, even when your body and brain are telling
you to stay.

JULY 31

Great Messages

Every sales representative must take inventory of their "personal tool kit" – the relationship selling skills you have honed to effectively sell your products and services. Consider these the tools for asking great questions, the tools to demonstrate great listening; tools to ensure a gentle education approach. And at a personal level assess: the tools of discipline; the tools of positive energy; the tools of interpersonal relationship building; the tools of personal organization; the tools of time management; and the tools of motivation. What tools do you have to utilize to their fullest advantage?

AUGUST 1

Internal Relationships

Making operational changes encourages the
medical staff to feel listened to and appreciated.
Tangible actions (e.g., ordering a new piece
of equipment, changing a rule, or adapting a
schedule) are also necessary to keep the business
you already receive. That's not growth – it's
maintenance, and it is important.

AUGUST 2

Strategic Sales

Each one of us has a role in achieving the ultimate goals of sales success. If we can all understand our own responsibilities in that process, then we have an organization with a chance to achieve the levels of success we all dream of.

AUGUST 3

Forward Thinking

Program momentum is aided by the ability to clearly state the facts. Be honest and forthright as program momentum comes about because everyone knows where they stand. The approach and method to accomplish this is customized to clearly state your style and approach. Define your approach.

AUGUST 4

Attitude

Practice fairness and patience upon yourself as you change, grow and earn more sales success. Sometimes we fall victim to things beyond our control, no matter how prepared we are, how hard we try, or how much we believe in ourselves. In being kind to our own selves, we may actually find the ability to rise from these internal sales challenges faster and not develop a "victim mentality."

AUGUST 5

Great Messages

For relationships to properly heal and develop, both parties involved must work to move beyond the problems at hand, to learn together and use past lessons to grow stronger together. The client will not initiate this so you and your organization must own the process.

AUGUST 6

Strategic Sales

The truly effective sales person directs the process of new business and relationships with an understanding that success is based on the accumulation of short-term and long-term victories.

AUGUST 7

Motivation

Education is wonderful, but there is plenty of knowledge without a purpose. Direction is necessary, but there are plenty of orders without plans. Talent is valuable, but there are plenty of gifted people without successful careers ... Live with a purpose. Attack it with passion. Commit to your own success.

AUGUST 8

Internal Relationships

Customer service is almost exclusively out of the hands of the representative. Frame this honestly and then rely on your internal team to make it happen.

AUGUST 9

Great Messages

The most frequently used tools are a single-page sheet with an article or brief, a segment for data, and updates related to access, technology, or people. It's easily updated and offers a nice leave-behind for the representative and a good follow-up tool to set the stage for the next visit. Is it time for you to update your tools?

AUGUST 10

Strategic Sales

Use time between visits to learn supplemental
facts based on the prospect's specific interests.
This detailed pre-call planning offers tremendous
opportunity to customize and add value. The
market is cluttered, you must differentiate to
progress the relationship.

AUGUST 11

Forward Thinking

Successful sales people do not just drop out of the sky, they evolve. A champion learns, prepares, watches, attempts, fails, picks themselves up, believes, wins, succeeds and then excels. It is a long, difficult process, and it has to be that way. Constant improvement will make you successful.

AUGUST 12

Attitude

Don't ever let fear of failure stop your pursuit. Fear is often an irrational thought process stemming from personal insecurity. We will always excel the quickest when we realistically understand our limitations, and then acquire the skills needed to conquer our sales fears.

AUGUST 13

Internal Relationships

The definition of a team is as follows: A group of committed individuals, with complementary skills who have ownership in common goals of performance, purpose, principles and direction. Teams should also have a process of individual responsibility and mutual accountability. Who should be on your team?

AUGUST 14

Strategic Sales

Never believe that doctors don't care about their patients' experience and your service as it relates to that experience.

AUGUST 15

Focus

Success is results, but it's also about focused work and "putting your nose to the grindstone." Talent, skills, and knowledge are great assets, but sometimes nothing can take the place of simply pushing through the daily challenges. What will you need to push through today?

AUGUST 16

Attitude

Problems and service issues are a reality for sales
staff. Take the time to listen, really listen to the
verbal and non-verbal messages. Sometimes we
need to ask the client, "What would you have me
do with this information?"

Impact

Creative thinking is the root of all success – if you do something with it.

AUGUST 18

Forward Thinking

In examining your personal sales direction, care
about your growth and how it can positively impact
the organization and your personal life. Care
enough to show your commitment. It will enhance
relationships externally and internally.

AUGUST 19

Strategic Sales

No matter how strongly you believe in your sales approach, even if you possess great knowledge and skills, someone will find fault or criticize. Don't let this bring you down, rise above it.

AUGUST 20

Internal Relationships

It is essential to have the ability to self-assess your own sales skills. When self-assessing, remember it is about the skills you need to meet the goals.

AUGUST 21

Attitude

One of the greatest challenges -- even before trying to implement a plan for sales growth -- is to trust your own instincts. If you cannot find yourself to be trust worthy, you will never be able to achieve sales success.

AUGUST 22

Strategic Sales

When difficulties arise in a sales setting, you simply can't abandon long-term perspectives for the short-term crises. Never sacrifice your goals for a quick-fix.

AUGUST 23

Focus

Focus time and energy where it matters most.
Don't get caught up in pointless tasks.

AUGUST 24

Great Messages

Create your method of communicating internally
that sales efforts are more art than science and
develop a culture of tolerance for new ideas
and suggestions.

AUGUST 25

Motivation

In your sales role, how do you exceed expectations of your prospects, your clients, and your internal stakeholders?

AUGUST 26

Forward Thinking

Never wish your way to sales success. You must work from a strategy, prepare your approach, commit and then execute. Consistent small steps will create the outcome you desire.

AUGUST 27

Strategic Sales

The meeting is not done when you leave the practice. Consider next steps and actions that will add value for the prospect and make the time they spent with you stand out.

AUGUST 28

Competition

A product pitch is never as strong as dialogue; it seldom has the ability to pull business away from a competing service. Take the relationship part of relationship sales seriously -- think about what works for them.

AUGUST 29

Great Messages

Get promises for sales differentiators. Ask the clincher questions internally – what can they promise to deliver? Access and time frame specifics should be detailed.

AUGUST 30

Strategic Sales

To be effective, you must take a strategic approach
to stand apart from other sales representatives.
You must provide a distinct level of information and
expertise to create a position of VALUE.

AUGUST 31

Great Messages

"How's it going?" rarely leads you to meaningful dialogue. Resolve today to find a meaningful method for initiating conversations.

SEPTEMBER 1

Impact

Spend time with the people who help you become a better sales person. It's not about them making you better because they will do something for you; it's about making you better because they help you see the possibilities you hold within. While you're at it, why not offer yourself as that type of person to another. We get back tenfold what we give to others.

Attitude

In a sales role there is no greater attitude than one of hope. If you believe there is a chance, no matter how slim the odds of reaching and achieving your goal, then it just might happen. Some representatives struggle to see the possibilities and opportunities which lie before them. The day you lose hope is the day you are through.

SEPTEMBER 3

Internal Relationships

"Under the radar" is a dangerous place for your role internally. Make sure your strategy for demonstrated internal value is getting good attention.

SEPTEMBER 4

Competition

Stay consistent in your message and meeting
frequency. It takes time to earn business
that is currently with a competitor and many
representatives give up too soon. Manage yourself
if you feel nervous about staying on one topic for
multiple visits and start flavor-of-the-month sales
instead. This is not a quick sale.

SEPTEMBER 5

Strategic Sales

In healthcare, the sales process occurs in small increments with the prospect expressing ongoing interest for moving the relationship forward. Layer clinical and organization value with the outcomes, get the people involved and then let the physician see how he or she will be a part of the process. If I can see myself in your process, you've earned the referral.

SEPTEMBER 6

Forward Thinking

Promote a culture that invests in learning about the prospect's world and their needs and explore collaboration early on. Creating credibility never happens overnight. What do you need to do to encourage this?

SEPTEMBER 7

Internal Relationships

Any plan by a sales representative, regardless of
its brilliant insight or universal support, cannot be
successfully implemented if there is not a process
in place. Recognition for success must be swift
and consistent.

SEPTEMBER 8

Strategic Sales

Success requires two steps. The first step is one that many representatives have; it's doing relationship building visits. The second step moves you beyond showing up. A sales strategy is formulated to effect changes in the prospect's referral behavior. Your sales success requires both willingness to do the visits and a strategy to earn the right business as a result.

SEPTEMBER 9

Focus

The most difficult aspect of focus is that it is lost in bits and pieces. Revisit your plan frequently and don't make excuses.

SEPTEMBER 10

Attitude

Your character is a compass providing you
with moral and ethical standards to guide and
direct you to the thoughts and behaviors needed
for healthy, functional, and successful sales
relationships. Never lose your compass.

SEPTEMBER 11

Motivation

Try to gain opportunities for one-on-one meetings as the norm, and use the group meetings only when you have someone to introduce or plan a formal presentation. Very different information is gained with a one-on-one. Group meetings are always about the task, never about personal motivations.

SEPTEMBER 12

Great Messages

Ask quality questions and clearly understand
the client or physician's needs. As you do, stand
prepared to disclose appropriate details about the
strategic direction when needed.

SEPTEMBER 13

Strategic Sales

Be the kind of representative that consistently delivers on the promises made. Value for the client comes from a relationship and understanding, not "tell and sell" or "find and fix".

Forward Thinking

The best physician relations programs generally
start with a clear sense of direction.

SEPTEMBER 15

Attitude

Find a support network of people who can offer you objective feedback. The last thing you need is a "yes person" – someone who will tell you that you are doing well even if they know you are not. They can't instill their vision upon you, but they can provide clarity via a fresh perspective.

Motivation

Be grateful for the difficulties you encounter on the road to sales success. Don't let those challenges cause you to quit. Never believe that only you suffer problems. Difficulties are part of sales, so strengthen your resolve and cement your commitment to rise above the clouds and feel the light of success on your face.

SEPTEMBER 17

Strategic Sales

Relationship sales experts appreciate the value of a good question. Instead of telling about your service or stating, "Do you have anything for me today?" frame an insightful question to learn more about their challenges. Or ask about future growth, "What affect do you believe the market challenges will have on you and your peers?" Dialogue is healthy.

SEPTEMBER 18

Great Messages

Consider that marketing to consumers and marketing to physicians are not mutually exclusive. Keep in touch with all the messages. Evaluate the messages through the filter of your prospective customer.

SEPTEMBER 19

Internal Relationships

When sales representatives fail to meet the organization's expectations, it is often because of one of two reasons. In one case, the goals are too broad and too vague. The second reason is that the representative is unsure about how to accomplish their job. Once you have found clarity, answer, "How am I going to accomplish this?"

SEPTEMBER 20

Strategic Sales

Are you in the right relationships? Assuming you created your prospect lists using a rigorous, data-driven process, you're likely seeing some results. Are you? And if you have been at it for a while, have you done an update of the target process?

SEPTEMBER 21

Attitude

Our industry is filled with people who believe their
position or status is an entitlement. They believe that
their failures are always someone else's fault. There
is no place for self-absorbed individuals who don't
care for anyone or anything except themselves.

SEPTEMBER 22

Strategic Sales

A great representative can predict the next statement that the prospect will make. But they pace the conversation to add that pause, or thoughtful comment, before the "big punch." Take a breath – it's good for you and it creates impact.

SEPTEMBER 23

Internal Relationships

While it is true that a salesperson must work to gain the respect of physicians on a constant basis, it is imperative for healthy, functional, working relationships that you are respectful of internal stakeholders. What does that mean? It means being courteous, polite, giving, open, and tolerant of the differences in their roles and their approach.

SEPTEMBER 24

Forward Thinking

The representative who defines their vision and establishes personal goals is taking charge of creating their own destiny. Another person can care about what happens to you, but they are not you. You are the Chief Executive Officer, Chairman of the Board, and President of your territory. You are, and always will be, the biggest shareholder in your life.

SEPTEMBER 25

Great Messages

Remember that the gatekeeper's job is to make certain the right people get through. How do you demonstrate that you are that "right person?"

Internal Relationships

Our ability to work better together internally
creates a better outcome for those with whom we
work for and those we have targeted.

SEPTEMBER 27

Leadership

It is valuable for the leaders of a team to have a blend of skills which, when combined, can lead others to success and excellence. The complementary nature of the staff and eclectic composition provides a healthy perspective for all team members.

SEPTEMBER 28

Forward Thinking

The road to sales success is not meant to be just hard work, challenges and commitment. Take time to witness the joy that this role has to offer. Enjoy today and remember your reward is not all found at the closing. Enjoy the journey.

SEPTEMBER 29

Great Messages

To earn new referrals we must treat prospects how
they want to be treated. While it sounds easy, it
requires that we put ourselves in their shoes --
and sometimes that's tough. Take the time today to
try it with one of those individuals that challenges
you most.

SEPTEMBER 30

Strategic Sales

Take the time to examine who you are as a person, then fully comprehend how you represent yourself in the methods and manner of a sales professional. Is your style compatible with the expectations of your organization? Is your style compatible with your clients?

OCTOBER 1

Internal Relationships

Step back and evaluate how you live the brand in daily interactions, both within the organization and as you work with prospects on growth.

OCTOBER 2

Attitude

Be an optimistic person. In doing so, you will see
the market, your prospects and envision your goal
to grasp all that is possible. The optimist knows
that with the bad, there is better; with pain, there
will be triumph; with failure, comes success.
Without embracing the philosophy of optimism,
you can never hope to find sales success.

OCTOBER 3

Leadership

Any sales leader must be able to mentor the most basic building blocks of relationships. They must be loyal, accepting, patient, respectful, trustworthy and caring. They must also be able to functionally communicate, live with integrity, and display a willingness to help others.

OCTOBER 4

Strategic Sales

A common pitfall is found in the lack of a structured program, combined with an unrealistic time frame for results. Be careful to not let the passion for immediate change replace the effort side and the long term relationship building that will stage your future growth.

OCTOBER 5

Internal Relationships

A team filled with finger-pointers and closed-door gossips is a team destined to implode upon itself from the weakness of its internal relationships.

OCTOBER 6

Attitude

As you progress down the path of sales success you will encounter plenty of doubters. Learn to respectfully ignore them. They may actually be a blessing in disguise as they will test the resolve of your vision. If you let them derail your strategy, then you probably are not ready to claim success as your own.

OCTOBER 7

Great Messages

Physicians want to know that representatives understand their practice. Make sure your conversations today call out something about their practice.

OCTOBER 8

Impact

Successfully growing referrals requires that you close the deal. And closing begins with understanding and working the process. There is no magical formula or perfect phrase.

OCTOBER 9

Forward Thinking

Road weary is a potential condition of this role.
Take the time to feed your soul. Stay healthy as
your physical and mental health translates into a
healthy sales attitude.

OCTOBER 10

Great Messages

Don't measure your greatness by the number of sales you had last quarter alone. Also consider the number of clients who continue to rely on you and your execution. They will be appreciative and understand your products and success.

OCTOBER 11

Strategic Sales

Remember this formula: a data driven strategy + a solid plan + differentiated products + consistent application of selling skills = sales success.

OCTOBER 12

Attitude

Resolve and determination are wonderful tools to posses, but one must also be aware of the time frame in solving problems. Not every issue is going to have a solution. Occasionally we must let go. Ask yourself this question: Is this an inconvenience and does it prevent referrals?

OCTOBER 13

Focus

While you are willing and able to manage multiple
work activities, this is not the real reason you were
hired. Authentic commitment to growing business
means a single-mindedness and concentration in
the field. Assess how your hours have been used
the last week. Does it support your field obligation?

OCTOBER 14

Strategic Sales

Make certain that the assumptions about large group behaviors match the way their referral decisions actually play out. Although large groups may have better internal communication, it is never safe to assume a conversation with one doctor is shared with others.

Internal Relationships

Programs that demonstrate consistent growth over time have a very intentional plan in place. What's your plan?

OCTOBER 16

Attitude

Pressure can be a motivator, but it can also have a negative impact. Pressure which challenges us is external. Pressure which destroys is internal. Assess the source of your pressure. A realistic expectation with a manageable level of pressure is the best recipe -- make a batch of that for healthier selling.

OCTOBER 17

Forward Thinking

WE DREAM! WE SEE! WE CREATE! WE DO! WE
SUCCEED!

OCTOBER 18

Attitude

Care about who you are and where you are going.
It is your destiny as well as your gift to this job.
Consider the impact you are having today and then
detail the impact you hope to have next year on this
date. Impact for the job and impact for you.

OCTOBER 19

Great Messages

Today, find an innovative way to engage the client in dialogue and increase their interest in your services.

OCTOBER 20

Forward Thinking

If the representative wants to be successful, they must create an approach that is focused on what prospects need. Meetings must follow up on past meetings and include good conversations about the doctors' expectations -- both for themselves and those they serve.

OCTOBER 21

Strategic Sales

To advance your relationship strategy within a group environment make certain you determine who the formal and informal group leaders are. Your message and approach will be different for each of them. Put together a list of internal advocates who may be helpful in determining this.

OCTOBER 22

Great Messages

The most effective approach is to stage your messages in a series of small specific focused topics that help minimize risk for the prospective physician and assist you in showing all aspects of your service.

OCTOBER 23

Motivation

Remember, you must work harder than the competition to earn referrals that are currently going elsewhere. Otherwise, it is not worth the risk for a prospect to change their existing referral pattern.

OCTOBER 24

Strategic Sales

Before you begin your sales calls today, take inventory of your advancement plans with each prospect. Do you have a real plan? Do you have good questions to ask? Frame the dialogue you hope to have and background to support it and your desired outcome. "Old timers" can get sloppy with pre-call planning. Sometimes you sneak by. Sometimes you pay the price.

OCTOBER 25

Forward Thinking

Have the courage to be a great student of the profession. Learn new things, try new techniques, do a self-assessment and write down your self-improvement goals.

OCTOBER 26

Great Messages

Be assertive, succinct, and prepared. You know the gatekeeper will ask why you need to see the prospect, so plan ahead. Customize your reply for each person. If you are speaking with a receptionist, your reply will be different than if you are speaking with an office manager or final decision maker.

OCTOBER 27

Strategic Sales

There are times when a new service requires a broad based announcement to every audience. A blitz of the market can work very nicely. Every customer gets contacted with the same message in a designated time period. As you consider blitzing the market with an announcement message, make sure your message is meaningful, brief, succinct and actionable. Don't use the "tell and promote" approach too often or you will wear out its impact.

OCTOBER 28

Competition

If you talk about superior attributes of your service,
make sure you can back it up with proof. If you
are uncertain, make today the day that you query
internal stakeholders to get that knowledge.

OCTOBER 29

Strategic Sales

We've all experienced that wonderful phenomenon when, after we've worked on a plan for days, we put it down for a day or two before returning to it. And when we do, it looks a little different. We attack it with a fresh perspective and find that the modifications we make create a better, stronger plan.

OCTOBER 30

Impact

As a field representative, you must first and foremost, be able to design a visit that leaves the physician feeling like they benefit. Make certain that beyond getting through the gatekeeper, you are the one that gets invited back.

OCTOBER 31

Great Messages

Great representatives recognize that you have a "can't afford to lose" group and find ways to be empathetic to the realities they face. Reflect on their needs and keep balance in the relationship beyond just asking them to support the organization's needs.

NOVEMBER 1

Internal Relationships

Is your program evolving with your organization?
Revitalize your efforts to gather nuggets of new
information that may impact your approach. This
includes sharing what you learn in the field in a way
that is meaningful to leaders. You can be sure that
they are on the lookout for new competitive angles.

NOVEMBER 2

Forward Thinking

We've all tried hard and yet plans did not go as we hoped. Pat yourself on the back for the effort, then try again. Success comes to those who stay the course, enhance the process and keep working with the client.

NOVEMBER 3

Attitude

Do you believe in yourself? Do you have the
courage to support and defend your expertise
to those who would want to deter or destroy your
confidence in your ability to earn new business,
and your sales strategy?

NOVEMBER 4

Great Messages

Issues are just part of the role. Successful representatives realize that they can acknowledge others' views, learn more about how they would like you to deal with the issue and present an action plan. None of this is about throwing your organization under the bus. Make sure that you stay neutral and don't take sides against your internal team.

NOVEMBER 5

Strategic Sales

What caring means to persons of character, is that they display themselves through acts of kindness, compassion and sharing. They do all they can to help others, and live "The Golden Rule." Caring people also understand that by having concern about their own direction and goals in life, they provide inspiration in their quest for sales success.

NOVEMBER 6

Forward Thinking

If you should get lost in the day-to-day issues of winning or losing, always return to your goals. What is the number one reason you were hired by the organization? The answer is the road map of clarity in the pursuit of success.

Strategic Sales

To be successful, the representative must clearly understand the prospect's needs from their perspective and the benefit your organization offers that can meet this need.

Great Messages

For a relationship to move forward, you must find a way to position what is positive. Rather than be frustrated by the lack of service for some areas, document the specifics, and include them in the regular report.

NOVEMBER 9

Attitude

Take care of your physical being. The ability to sell,
think on your feet and meet internal expectations
can be best performed by those individuals who
also maintain physical health. The body and mind
work in unison for the good of the whole.

NOVEMBER 10

Competition

If you have pure differentiation, something that nobody can compete with, then leverage it big time. In this case it is about leveraging momentum. Spread the word.

NOVEMBER 11

Great Messages

If you are in a practice that is short on the happiness factor, make sure you understand why. Manage your enthusiasm so you are not over the top, but don't be afraid to share a nice dose of warmth while you are there.

NOVEMBER 12

Strategic Sales

You can experience all the training possible
in product knowledge, sales skills, time-
management, organizational approach,
relationship building and still never be completely
prepared. Why? Because many sales scenarios
require an instinctive response. Learning from
your experiences and the experiences of others
you will flourish.

NOVEMBER 13

Forward Thinking

Be willing to acquire the tools needed to achieve personal success. Not everyone has been given everything they need in order to accomplish all they dream of. Don't blame others and don't let it serve as an anchor keeping you where you are instead of where you hope to go.

NOVEMBER 14

Great Messages

The representative role is not to pitch and not to
interrogate, but rather to ask informed questions
and listen for clues. Be willing to say,
"Tell me more."

NOVEMBER 15

Strategic Sales

The best representatives find creative methods
and design systematic tools to keep apprised of
their team's level of effectiveness in the field.

NOVEMBER 16

Attitude

What does it take to be a great sales person?
It begins with supporting and protecting your
organization. It requires staying informed, sharing,
obeying and playing by the rules. To go past
good to get to great requires being accountable,
responsible, respectful and clear on what the
client needs.

NOVEMBER 17

Great Messages

Anyone can find excuses for why not. Giving in to a gatekeeper, or finding reasons why the competition is on top is easy. Those who excel in this role bury the excuses under their passion to succeed.

NOVEMBER 18

Focus

Work on keeping concentration and focus on
your sales strategy today. Sales focus means
that we create an environment that requires and
allows the representative to be in the field. You are
responsible for your own focus.

NOVEMBER 19

Motivation

It's not uncommon for field staff to get
discouraged, disgruntled and even inactive
if they're not feeling or seeing progress with
their visits. Take time to sort through the various
layers of these relationships to find opportunities
to restore some of the basics. You can't stay in
negative space very long and generally few others
can move you out of it. Personal power for this one.

NOVEMBER 20

Great Messages

Relationship sales start with learning about physicians' needs. The approach and message should not be "we have," but rather, "you need."

NOVEMBER 21

Strategic Sales

In your pursuit of success, take the time to really
assess the type of prospects you have. Evaluate
their needs, and then create your sales plan before
implementing your field tactics. The day is long
past where a representative can make a pitch to
the prospect and get an instant "yes."

NOVEMBER 22

Internal Relationships

Internal integration really matters. Frankly, it requires a willingness to take the plunge and create the relationship if one does not already exist.

NOVEMBER 23

Attitude

It is quite common to hear individuals make excuses about the propensity for certain individuals to have all the luck in the world while they have none. Luck and good fortune are directly proportionate to the degree of hard work those same people contribute to their cause. Usually, the people who claim that others get more than their share of luck are the same people who wait for money to grow on trees. Work as hard as you can and you will be amazed at the good fortune and success that will come to you.

NOVEMBER 24

Great Messages

Hearing is not listening. As you work with your
prospects today really listen with your mind free
of distraction. Pay attention to their body language
and really concentrate on what they are saying
rather than what you want them to say next.

NOVEMBER 25

Strategic Sales

Problems must be solved on a daily basis, but they must be solved with a resolute eye on the horizon. Have faith in your process.

NOVEMBER 26

Internal Relationships

If you can't support the vision that other members have created for your sales effort, it is your responsibility to tell the others about your feelings. As you do recognize that it is a battle you may not win, but ignoring it will not make it go away.

NOVEMBER 27

Attitude

The complex world of earning credibility for a
representative means that the relationship side is
front and center and it is augmented with the brief
"tell" messages and not the other way around.

Great Messages

A key to successful relationship-selling with long-term value is the ability to be consistent. A consistent message, approach, style, and regularity of meetings all make the difference.

NOVEMBER 29

Impact

The journey to sales success is a difficult one indeed. As we discipline ourselves to hold fast to the process, we must also find the time to celebrate small victories and enjoy the trip. Appreciate the ride because if you don't, you might never realize it when you finally get to the top.

NOVEMBER 30

Strategic Sales

If faced with the choice of perfection or consistency from any sales team, always choose consistency. Perfection is impossible and causes far too much stress and anxiety on the human psyche to reach for such an illusion. Consistency is a commitment to perform at a level you are capable of, and do so with relative frequency. It is totally possible and far less taxing on your mind.

DECEMBER 1

Forward Thinking

It's easy to get caught up in the priorities of the day when business is moving at lightning speed. Recognize that keeping your program current can be as important as most anything you have on your plate. So, start with just one piece. Get down to the tactical layer to allow your modifications and new ideas to be tangible and something you can use today.

DECEMBER 2

Great Messages

Old messages may need a make-over. Today is the day to find a new way to introduce your bread and butter service. Perhaps it starts with probing their current situation in more detail.

DECEMBER 3

Strategic Sales

Sometimes the best way to get your mind off the
problems you have is to consider the problems
that other people have. We have a tendency to
spend so much time obsessing about our world
that we ignore the issues of others --
including the practice.

DECEMBER 4

Attitude

Do not make excuses or blame others for your mistakes and misfortunes. Concern yourself with examining the actions which caused such problems to occur. In a sales setting, don't blame others. Get innovative and find other ways to meet your goals.

DECEMBER 5

Forward Thinking

You cannot sustain success by simply knowing and being committed to your vision. Success demands that you demonstrate the right foundation. You will be remembered for what you have accomplished. You will be honored for what you have overcome. You will be revered for the principles you have lived by.

DECEMBER 6

Great Messages

Pay attention to the self-appointed leader in the group meeting, but also to those who are quiet. Seek them out and learn their thoughts and needs with a one-on-one conversation.

DECEMBER 7

Internal Relationships

Have you been asked to sell a product that you lack confidence in? You have only two options. 1) Do research to affirm its sales readiness. 2) Talk to your internal stakeholders and move it off your list. This, of course, only happens when the evidence supports your concern.

DECEMBER 8

Great Messages

The role of fairness within any relationship means that each and every person is treated with the utmost dignity and equality.

DECEMBER 9

Strategic Sales

People like to be around others like them. Pay attention today to the personality and attributes of those you meet. Match your style, your tone and your approach. It will make a difference.

DECEMBER 10

Competition

Your time with the prospect is limited, so don't let
the noise and distraction in your brain keep you
from listening to the real message and client need.

Great Messages

After a group meeting you should do individual follow-up meetings with attendees; it's a good chance to add information or answer questions prospects might have.

DECEMBER 12

Strategic Sales

There is one very important consideration in sales direction change -- not everyone is going to be thrilled about the future vision. Change means altering, shifting and sacrificing. Not everyone involved is going to feel that same passion for change. It is their right to feel the way they do. For this very reason, people affected by the change must have, or be willing to develop, ownership of the process. Without such ownership, significant or lasting change will not occur.

DECEMBER 13

Forward Thinking

A little memo for next year's plan: "Define my
vision of sales excellence and what details will be
required so I can make it happen."

DECEMBER 14

Attitude

Do not waste your time judging accomplishments or problems of other representatives. The reality is that you probably will never know the particulars of their approach, so it becomes a drain on your energy and time, which could be put to better use on your own sales goals.

DECEMBER 15

Great Messages

In a healthy, character-driven relationship, control flows freely between the representative and the client. Both parties have a right and a responsibility to control or guide communications. With such a functional system, either party is willing to let the other lead at various times, or to follow as the situation dictates.

DECEMBER 16

Leadership

As a sales leader, carve out opportunities for personal connections with others in your organization. When they know you and they understand your motives you minimize the risk of sabotage and enhance the opportunity for collaboration. It all makes sense - you benefit when they support your vision for growth.

DECEMBER 17

Competition

Be nice. A great competitive strategy is to be nice. Work to accommodate the staff's needs, be flexible when you can, and when they need a favor try to provide it. In the retail world, lack of attentiveness to a customer's needs costs as much as two-thirds of repeat business.

DECEMBER 18

Great Messages

It is critically important that the representative knows how to ask about the prospect's needs and then has the ability to listen, comprehend and reply. Consider one new question today, then test it and see what you learn.

DECEMBER 19

Attitude

Being courageous means taking risks, taking
chances and potentially falling down. Personal
fortitude does not insure immediate success, but
it does provide immediate insight in determining
who you currently are and what you ultimately have
the potential to accomplish.

DECEMBER 20

Forward Thinking

Where will your program be in two years? It's
never too early to start planning for the future.
Carve out some time to think about what needs to
happen to launch your program to the next level.

DECEMBER 21

Great Messages

Be respectful of the gatekeeper's role. If the gatekeeper is also the office manager, meet with him or her and learn about their role. Find ways to value and assist them to meet their needs.

DECEMBER 22

Strategic Sales

Think and act creatively, professionally, and respectfully and you will outsmart and out sell your competition every time.

DECEMBER 23

Motivation

When teaching and enriching skills to nurture relationships don't forget the M E principle.

Motivate -- Encourage physician's involvement and ownership. Educate-- Assist physicians and their team in understanding how you can support their needs. Entertain -- The process of knowledge accumulation should also be fun.

DECEMBER 24

Internal Relationships

The power found within any successful sales person is in part a result of the health and functionality of their internal relationships. What do you need to do today to enhance your internal credibility?

DECEMBER 25

Great Messages

Relationships should be in existence to assist us all in becoming better people and in reaching new heights in our sales relationships. The bottom line is that a healthy relationship enhances our enjoyment in the sales role and advances our success. Good relationships provide us with the energy and support to be the best we can be.

DECEMBER 26

Internal Relationship

Any plan by a sales representative, regardless
of its brilliant insight or universal support,
cannot be successfully implemented if there
is not a process in place.

DECEMBER 27

Great Messages

Trust is a two-way street in physician relationships. You must be trustworthy and the physician needs to take what is being said at face value. Work to earn a trust based relationship that makes truth a comfortable option. You may find those who have a hidden agenda or those who are suspect. This makes it difficult to move them forward. Assume the best and manage the others.

DECEMBER 28

Strategic Sales

You can keep the business you have by being as
good as the competition, but you cannot grow
new business unless there is something that
differentiates it.

Great Messages

Sales matches the needs of the customer with the benefits of the product offered. Successful relationship sales programs have taken the sales process and customized it.

DECEMBER 30

Attitude

Another successful year is behind you. Reflect on all the good works that you have completed. When all the systems and processes are boiled down, sales success is still more a reflection of your attitude than anything else. The secret of success is found in the attitude of your pursuit.

Take a moment just to enjoy!
Tomorrow is a brand new year.

-- END --

DECEMBER 31

About the Author

Kriss Barlow, RN, MBA, has spent her entire professional career in the healthcare industry.

Kriss, who earned a bachelor's degree in nursing from Augustana College, Sioux Falls, SD, and a master of business administration degree from the University of Nebraska, is a principal of Barlow/McCarthy, a solutions-driven hospital-physician consulting group. She focuses on hospital-physician strategy, business solutions, and relationship and retention models.

A well-known health care expert, Kriss is a frequent speaker whose presentations are full of real, proven examples from her vast experience that inform and educate.

Kriss is the author of HealthLeader's Media books, The Complete Guide to Physician Relationships in an Accountable Care Era, A Marketer's Guide to Physician Relations, and co-author of Physician Relations Today: A Model for Growth.

When Kriss isn't working, she's enjoying her family life. Her husband, Doug, is the steadying force in her life and her biggest supporter. They have three fabulous sons, two charming daughters-in-law and a growing number of adorable grandchildren.